SHARING CULTURE
ULURU

Written & Photographed by STANLEY BREEDEN

Steve Parish
PUBLISHING

CONTENTS

Left: Ulu<u>r</u>u rises 348 metres from the plain. The lines of sand dunes that snake towards the monolith were shaped by southerly winds about 30 000 years ago.

ULURU AND KATA TJUTA

Australia's dry centre is dominated by seemingly endless plains and ridges of sandhills. Scattered through these vast lands are mountain ranges and gigantic rocky outcrops.

The predominant colour is red – red rocks and red sand. Of all the monolithic outcrops, none are more startling or imposing in size and rounded shape than Uluru and Kata Tjuta. They stand almost at the exact centre of the continent. The tallest is Mount Olga, which is 546 metres high. Mount Olga is one of the many domes that make up Kata Tjuta, which, in the local Aboriginal language, means "many heads".

Above: Kata Tjuta. The highest dome, on the left, is Mt Olga, 546 metres tall.

About 25 kilometres away stands the single, massive eminence of Uluṟu. It is 348 metres high and 9 kilometres in circumference. Both places have sacred caves, rocks and pools on their slopes and hidden in their dark crevices.

Uluṟu and Kata Tjuṯa are so noble and entrancing, so striking and revered, that they have become important national symbols for all Australians. Indeed, this place has been given World Heritage listing to recognise its cultural and natural importance to the whole world.

Pages 6 and 7: From the distance Uluṟu looks blue, but its rock is coloured earth red. The sand dune in the foreground has been rippled by the wind.

The almost constant wind has swept the sand of the plains into row upon row of dunes. Sand by itself is not a fertile, water-holding soil, but Uluru and Kata Tjuta are not in a true desert.

While some droughts may last several years, there are also times of plenty when one year of good rainfall follows another. Just once in a while there are floods.

During drought, when plants dry out and few animals are seen, the land looks barren. But a rich variety of plants has adapted to the sandy soil and erratic rainfall. There are ancient, hardy trees, tough, woody shrubs, and the short-lived flowering plants that spring up after rain.

Probably the most common and best-known plants from central Australia are the grasses known as spinifex. They are also called Porcupine Grasses. The rounded clumps have sharp, spiny blades that point outwards like the quills of a porcupine. Spinifex is dry and resinous, and few animals can digest it.

Above: A rain shower has deepened the colour of this sand dune. Kata Tjuta is on the horizon.

Right: *Lungkata*, the Blue-tongued Lizard, among wildflowers.

Pages 10 and 11: Billy Wara, an Anangu elder, lives close to Uluru.

From a distance, Uluṟu and Kata Tjuṯa look equally red and equally smooth – yet they are made of different kinds of rock. Both kinds are sedimentary rocks that were laid down between 550 and 500 million years ago. The sediments came from mountains that were eroding. These mountains may have been 3000 metres high. The sediments, from boulders to pebbles and from sand to mud, were carried down rivers and came to rest in alluvial fans on the plain. The finest

Above: Uluṟu's sandstone was laid down in strata. The layers, which tilted 90° during periods of mountain building, are very obvious in this photograph.

materials, the sand and mud, were carried further than the boulders and pebbles.

About 400 million years ago, these sediments began to metamorphose into rock. Then, for a long, long time the forces in the earth pushed and turned the rocks to build mountains.

Uluru, which is about 25 kilometres from the original source, is made up of sand and mud metamorphosed into a sandstone called arkose.

Above: **Close-up of Uluru's sandstone.**

The original sediments settled in layers, or strata, that can still be seen in the rock. The layered rock was subjected to enormous pressures and was tilted. Now the strata are at right angles to the plain. Some layers were softer than others, and so they have been eroded more deeply. These grooves carry rain as it runs off the rock.

Kata Tjuṯa, closer to the original mountains – which disappeared long ago – is made of a coarse rock called conglomerate. It includes sand and mud as well as pebbles and boulders up to one and a half metres in diameter. Rain, and the stress and strain caused by the big temperature changes between night and

Above: Olga Gorge at Kata Tjuṯa. Kata Tjuṯa is made up of a rock called conglomerate.

day, have eroded Uluṟu and Kata Tjuṯa into smooth, rounded shapes.

Erosion never stops. It goes on today. In central Australia, erosion produced mostly sand – more sand than can possibly be imagined. Nearly the whole of the centre is covered by it. In the process, huge amounts of oxidised iron were also released. This red oxide is what colours the rock and sand.

The sand was blown into lines of dunes by constant strong winds during a very dry time some 30 000 years ago. Archeologists think that Aṉangu first arrived at Uluṟu not long after this.

Pages 16 and 17: **After heavy winter rains, the dunes and plains are covered with flowers.**

Uluru, Kata-Tjuta and the plains around them are the home of the Pitjantjatjara and the Yankunytjatjara people. They call themselves Anangu, which means "the people".

Anangu have lived here for tens of thousands of years. They are connected to their land, the plants and animals through *Tjukurpa*. *Tjukurpa* is many things. It is the time of creation when heroic ancestral beings made the land. It is the law that governs and guides all the people's actions.

Above: Rhonda's father, Ivan, takes her out bush to teach her about the land.

It is the life force joining the people to the natural world. Ceremony and sacred places make the people one with *Tjukurpa*.

Because of *Tjukurpa*, Anangu know their lands so well that they can always find food and water, even during drought.

They lived well in good times. More importantly, they survived in the harshest years, even in the days before they owned cars and rifles, or had a supermarket to shop at. Everything they needed for body and spirit they found in the land.

Above: Anangu elders dig for *Maku*, witchetty grubs.
When the elders were young, Anangu lived in the bush for long periods.

Anangu at Uluru–Kata Tjuta live in one of the world's most beautiful and exciting places.

Anangu own the land. But they know that this place is important to other Australians as well, and they are very happy to share it with visitors from all over the world – more than 400 000 come every year. Anangu generously share much of their culture with all of these visitors.

Tony Tjamiwa says: "Our purpose is to

Above: Hundreds of thousands of visitors come to Uluru each year. Some rush from one place to another – they do not even pause to enjoy the beauty of Uluru in the afternoon light. Anangu call these *Minga*, ants.

explain and clarify our understanding of our world so that others can understand".

While they do not absolutely forbid it, Anangu do not like visitors to climb Uluru, their sacred rock.

Above: Visitors on the *Mala* Walk gather around a Ranger who is talking about Anangu culture.

ANANGU SPEAK OF ULURU

Tony Tjamiwa:

"That's a really important, sacred thing that you are climbing…you shouldn't climb. It's not the real thing about this place. The real thing is listening to everything. Listening and understanding everything. When we say don't climb, maybe that makes you a bit sad. But, anyway, that's what we are obliged to say. And all the tourists will brighten up and say: 'Oh, I see. This is the right way. This is the proper way. No climbing'."

Above: On the *Liru* Walk, Anangu show how to make resin from spinifex.

Barbara Tjikatu adds:

"If you worry about Aboriginal Law, leave it; don't climb it. You should think about *Tjukurpa* and stay on the ground. Please don't climb."

Instead of climbing Uluru, Anangu urge visitors to go on the *Mala* and *Liru* Walks, which are guided by Anangu and other rangers. They tell visitors about the landscape, its history and its culture. A visit to the cultural centre will add to everyone's knowledge and enjoyment.

Above: **A Ranger tells the story of the pythons and the venomous snakes.**

GATHERING FOOD

Imagine you found yourself somewhere at Uluṟu–Kata Tjuṯa, on foot, with your family, and you had to live there. What would you do? Where would you find food and water? How would you make fire once your matches ran out?

Unless you were Aṉangu and knew the country well, knew its secrets through *Tjukurpa*, you would not survive. Nor could you be expected to, for *Tjukurpa* takes a lifetime to learn.

Aṉangu do not just survive. They live

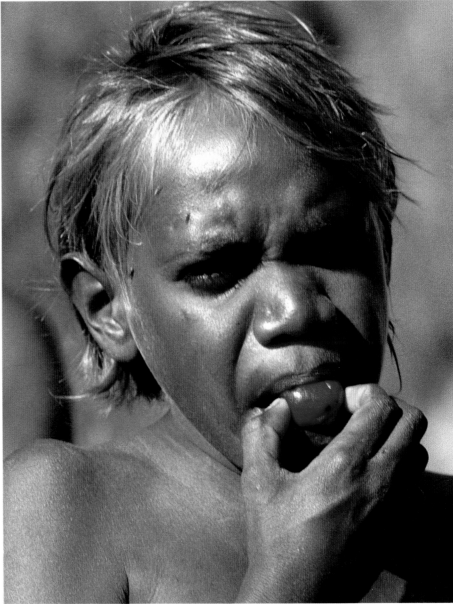

Left: *Mangaṯa*, quandong tree, bright with with ripe fruit.

Right: Daniel bites into a quandong, rich in Vitamin C.

happy, satisfying lives in the bush.

A family with a few *kuḻaṯa*, spears, *wana*, digging sticks, *kaḻi*, boomerangs, and *piti*, wooden dishes, will walk confidently into the bush and gather enough for everyone to eat in a few hours.

Without matches, they can make a fire in seconds. Water lies in pools around the bases of Uluṟu and Kata Tjuṯa.

Left: Elizabeth and Katy gather *Kampuṟarpa*, Bush Tomatoes.

Right: A handful of *Kampuṟarpa*.

Dotted throughout the surrounding country are small rock holes (see page 59) filled with water. These must be looked after all the time so they do not fill up with sand.

Just about everyone knows where the *Mangata*, the quandong tree, grows and when the nutritious fruit are ripe. The tasty *Kampurarpa*, the Bush Tomatoes, can be gathered from their small bushes after winter rain.

Wakalpuka, a kind of wattle, produces masses of seeds that are ground into flour to make bread.

These are just a few of the fruits and seeds that Anangu harvest.

Above: Barbara Tjikatu picks seed pods from *Wakalpuka*, a kind of wattle.

Top: *Wakalpuka* seed pods.

Bottom: The seeds are separated from the pods and then ground into a kind of flour.

Pages 28 and 29: Anangu children suck the nectar from *Kaliny-kaliny*, Honey Grevillea, flowers. Kata Tjuta is in the background.

FOR A SWEET TOOTH

Most children like sweet things to eat. In spring, A<u>n</u>angu children suck the nectar straight from the flowers of *Kaliny-kaliny*, the Honey Grevillea.

The nectar from these flowers is also an important part of the diet of many birds in central Australia.

Above: **Christopher is especially fond of nectar.**

Left: The fruit of the Ruby Saltbush are sweet and juicy.

Right: *Ili*, the Rock Fig, grows around the base of Ulu_r_u. A_n_angu love its ripe red fruit.

The children ask their grandparents to dig deep holes to take *Tjaḻa*, the Honey Ants, from their nests. These too are sweet.

Above: Maureen Natjuna had to dig deep to reach the nest of *Tjaḻa*, the Honey Ants.

Right: *Tjaḻa*, swollen with honey, stored on a piece of bark for Maureen's grandchildren.

The men hunt for *Malu*, the Red Kangaroo, sometimes following the tracks of a mob across the plains for hours.

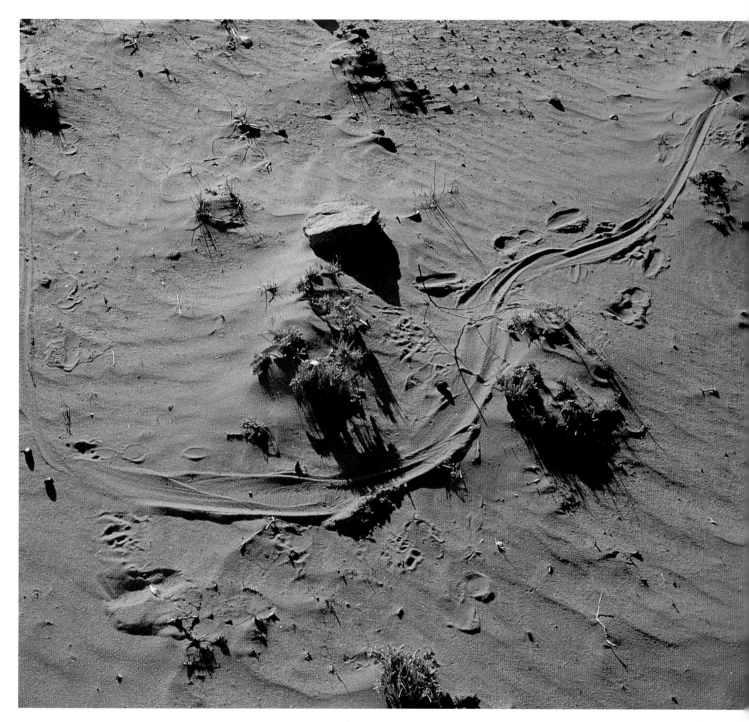

Left: Billy Wara likes to hunt *Malu*, the Red Kangaroo.   Above: *Malu*'s tracks.

The women dig delicious foods from the ground. *Milpali*, the Sand Goanna or monitor, is a favourite.

Most prized of all are *Maku*, witchetty grubs, the silky, white caterpillars of a giant moth. They are dug out of the roots of the *Ilykuwara* bush, which is a type of wattle.

Above: *Milpali*, the Sand Goanna, is a favourite food. Anangu dig them from their burrows.

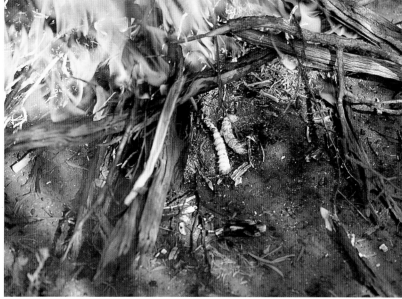

Top: **Manu and his mother dig for** *Maku,* **witchetty grubs.**   Bottom right: *Maku* **roasting in the fire.**

Bottom left: **The grubs are soft and smooth to the touch.**

TRACKS AND TRACKING

The animals write the story of everything they do across the dunes and plains. A̲nangu are experts at reading these stories.

By just glancing at a track, they know which type of animal made it, where it was going and what it was doing. Every morning, before the wind wipes away the tracks, A̲nangu can read what exciting things happened during the night.

They can see how a gecko caught a beetle; where a python tracked down and overpowered a bush rat; how fast a kangaroo had to hop to get away from pursuing dingos…

Above: *Ngiyari*, the Thorny Devil, leaves his tracks in the sand.

TJUKURPA STORIES

Uluru and Kata Tjuta bear the marks made by ancestral beings during the creation period of *Tjukurpa*.

Many stories about the creation and the sacred places nearby can only be told to people who have been through ceremonial business. But others can be told to everyone. Two such stories follow.

Please note that these stories form part of the Yankunytjatjara and Pitjantjatjara cultural property, and that they may not be used or reproduced in any form without the written permission of senior Anangu custodians.

The stories about Kata Tjuta are to do with men's ceremonial business and must remain secret.

Above: **Tracks on a sand dune.**

Pages 40 and 41: **There are many *Tjukurpa* stories associated with Uluru.**

KUNIYA AND THE *LIRU*

A young male Woma Python, a *Kuniya*, offended a group of *Liru*, venomous snakes. Some *Liru* came towards Uluṟu from the west, looking for the young *Kuniya* to punish him. The *Liru* found him, curled up asleep at the base of Uluṟu. They hurled spears at him and killed him. Many spears missed their target. They were thrown with such force that they made holes in the rock that are still there.

The killing of the young *Kuniya* enraged his aunt, a much larger python. She came underground from the other side of Uluṟu and confronted the raiders. The *Liru* laughed at her, mocking her. The huge *Kuniya*'s anger went out of control. She raced across Uluṟu's surface and killed one of the *Liru*. Such was her speed, she left a dark line across Uluṟu's surface.

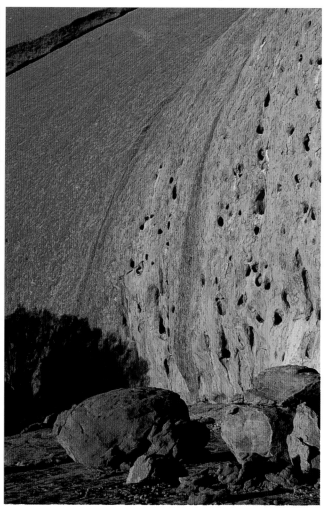

Top left: *Kuniya*, the Woma Python.

Bottom left: A King Brown Snake, one of the *Liru*.

Above right: Holes in the rock left by the *Liru*'s spears.

Right: The sinuous path left by the *Kuniya* when she chased the *Liru* can still be seen on Uluṟu.

THE *PANPANPALALA* AND *LUNGKATA*

One morning two *Panpanpalala*, Crested Bellbird, brothers went out hunting. They found the tracks of *Kalaya*, the emu. They began tracking it. Moving slowly and quietly, they came so close to *Kalaya* that they could spear it. One spear went right through the big bird, yet it did not die. It ran away. The brothers lost its tracks.

Lungkata, the Blue-tongued Lizard, was out hunting that same morning. He saw the wounded *Kalaya* and killed it for himself. He immediately cut the bird into pieces, built a fire and began to cook the meat.

Top: A Crested Bellbird feeds her chicks.

Bottom: *Lungkata*, the Blue-tongued Lizard.

Right: *Kalaya*, the emu.

Kalaya really belonged to the *Panpanpalala* brothers and *Lungkata* knew it was wrong to steal it.

The brothers soon found *Kalaya's* tracks again and followed them to *Lungkata's* cooking fire. Frightened, *Lungkata* ran away, dropping pieces of meat all over the ground. He scrambled up Uluru to his camp in a cave high on the rock. The *Panpanpalala* brothers built a fire beneath the cave. The smoke and heat made *Lungkata* dizzy and he fell to his death. The pieces of *Kalaya* meat and *Lungkata's* broken body turned to stone and can be seen at the base of Uluru.

Above left: **Tony Tjamiwa, an elder, tells some of the** *Tjukurpa* **stories.**

Above right: *Kalaya's* **leg, turned to stone.**

Above: The loose rocks at the base of Uluṟu are the remains of *Lungkaṯa*'s broken body.

Pages 48 and 49: The mysterious and sacred domes of Kata Tjuṯa glow at sunset. Uluṟu is in the distance.

Anangu children's classrooms have always been in the bush, among the rocks and sandhills. The teachers are their parents, grandparents, aunts and uncles. The children are taught where to find water, how to dig out *Maku*, the witchetty grub, when and where to find fruits, and how to make implements. They learn by doing, by being in their country.

The children must learn how to follow tracks. One of the most accomplished trackers and teachers is Edith Imantura

Above: Billy Wara tells his granddaughter how he made a *kulata*, or spear.

Richards. She points out the special points about the tracks left by each animal, how long ago they were there and where they were going. She makes marks in the sand with her hands to show what the tracks of particular animals look like.

The children learn about *Tjukurpa*.

They must learn the songs and dances for *inma*, ceremonies. The girls are painted for the *Kuniya*, python, *inma* and learn the steps. The boys act the story of *Lungkata*, the Blue-tongued Lizard.

Left: **Edith teaches Nyinku (right) about tracking.**

Top right: **Edith points out the tracks of birds.**

Bottom right: **She makes a perfect set of dingo tracks with her fingers.**

Anangu elders say: "We want to keep *Tjukurpa* strong. For us the past and present are one.

"These stories from the creative time of *Tjukurpa*, we bring them alive in our ceremony, our *inma*. It is our duty to look after *Tjukurpa*; it provides us with our reason for living. Our Law is how it should be.

"These are important *inma* and teach young people to keep the Law properly in their hearts and minds."

Above: **Girls learn the *Kuniya*, Woma Python, dance.**

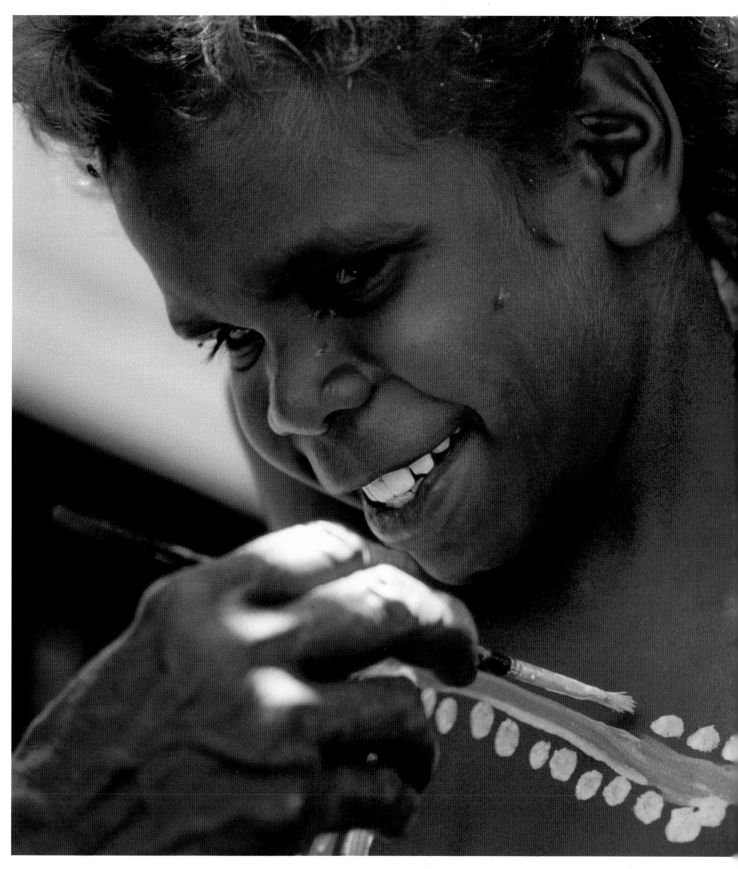

Above: The adults paint the children for the ceremonial dances. It is all part of teaching them the *inma*, or ceremonies.

Pages 54 and 55: Judy Trigger teaches the *Kuniya* dance.

When the children go out to play they are never far from the watchful eyes of an adult.

The children like to draw in the sand of the plains. They may imagine what a *Mamu* looks like, and then draw it. But they are only guessing, because *Mamus*, horrible monsters that are said to come out after dark to frighten children, are invisible to A̲nangu.

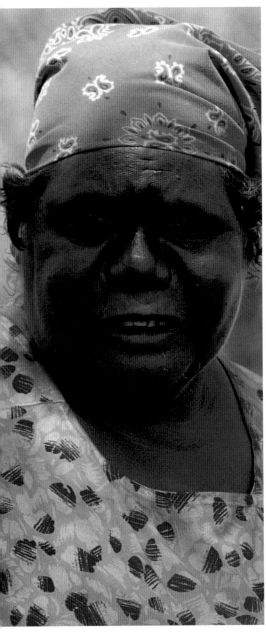

Left: Barbara Tjikatu keeps a watchful eye on the children.

Right: Daniel draws what he thinks a *Mamu* looks like.

DINGOS

The children often watch animals, like young dingos playing among the spinifex. Dingos, called *Papa*, can see *Mamu* spirits and may warn people of their presence.

A̱nangu sometimes take dingo pups from their den and then raise them to be hunting dogs.

Above: **Young dingos play among the spinifex.**

Rain, especially heavy rain, completely changes the sand and rocks as well as the plants and animals. The sand soaks up even the heaviest downpours without any run-off, and turns a darker red.

The rocks, too, turn darker. Unlike the sand dunes, their colour loses some of its brightness. The sandstone soaks up only a little rain. During heavy falls, streams of water tumble down grooves and run from one rock pool to another. Millions of years of rain have carved both the grooves and the pools.

Below the rocks, the water runs into

Above: Plants mature quickly after rain and their fruit are then ready for harvest.

ponds that overflow into creeks whose waters soon drain away in the sand.

In central Australia there are frogs that can sit dormant under ground through years of drought. Rain nudges them awake. They emerge and gather around water to sing and spawn. Insects swarm.

Rain in winter and spring germinates the seeds of annual plants that grow into fields of flowers – yellow, pink and white splashed with red and blue. Summer rain makes grass grow tall and thick, but few wildflowers spring up.

Left: During dry times there is no surface water. But Anangu know where there are wells in the rocks like this one. They can always find water.

Right: When it rains, water rushes down Uluru, filling pools at its base.

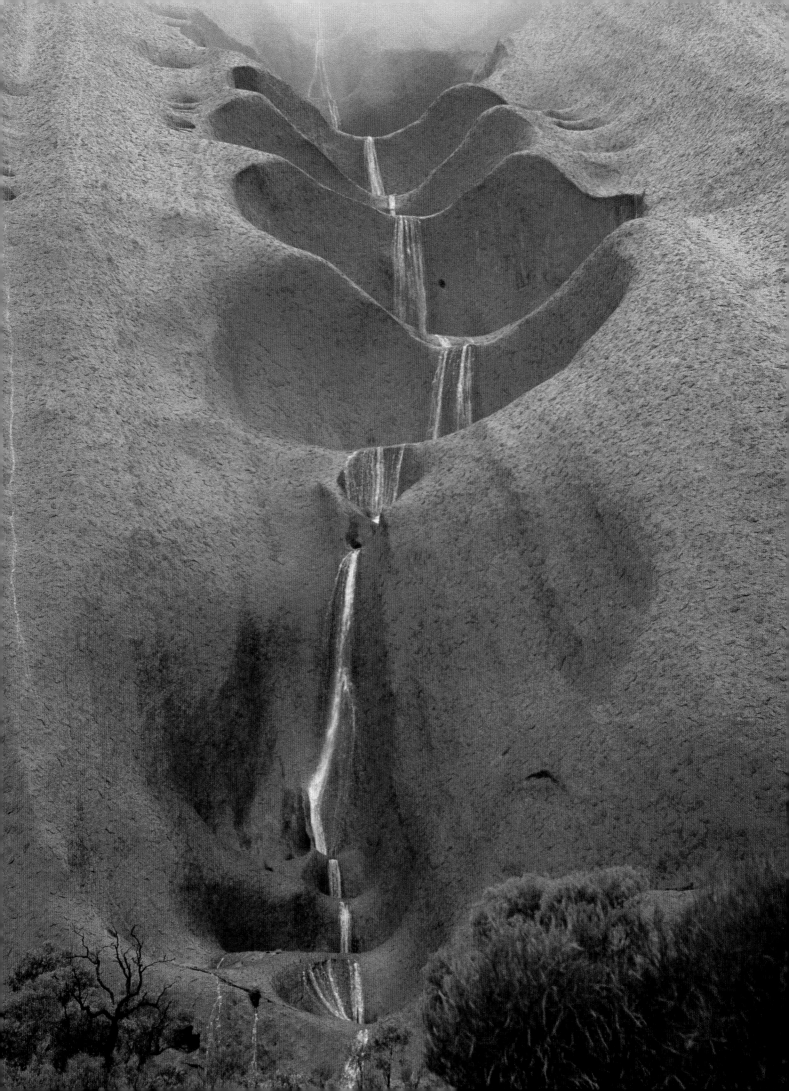

Left: A rivulet cascades from one water-sculptured pool to the next.

Top: A Trilling Frog. After heavy rain, frogs come to the pools to spawn.

Bottom: Raindrops on Desert Fringe Myrtle flowers.

Pages 62 and 63: Butter-yellow Saltspoon Daisies and brilliant purple parakeelya flourish after rain.

Fire, well-managed by Anangu in ways laid down in *Tjukurpa*, is needed to look after the country. To Anangu, well-cared-for country is a patchwork of regrowth and places ready to be burnt. This patchwork grows the most different plants, which then supports the greatest variety of animals.

Anangu know what and when to burn to make this patchwork. The spinifex is an indicator: when their clumps cover the plains and dunes, and when their centres begin to die, Anangu know the spinifex needs to be burnt back.

A calm winter's day is the best: then the fires do not race out of control. They move slowly, and animals can get away from the flames. At night a winter fire will die down or go out altogether, and so small burnt areas form a patchwork over the plains.

On hot, windy summer days, fires move fast, destroying everything in their path. Countless animals are killed. Plants that would survive winter fires also die. Summer fires burn all night across vast stretches of land. There is no patchwork.

After winter fires, perennial plants soon sprout again. The seeds of annuals lie ready to germinate as soon as rain falls.

Left: Hot summer fires consume all before them.

Above: Norman Tjakilyiri sets controlled winter fires that form a patchwork of burnt and unburnt country, providing the greatest diversity of plants and animals.

During a sunny spring after a rainy winter, Uluṟu–Kata Tjuṯa National Park is one of the most dazzlingly colourful places on earth. In just weeks, bare sandhills and plains change into fields of flowers that stretch to the horizon.

Winter can be cold. Reptiles and insects lie dormant in caves or in burrows in the sand. Spring sunshine coaxes them out into the warmth. Insects gnaw on leaves,

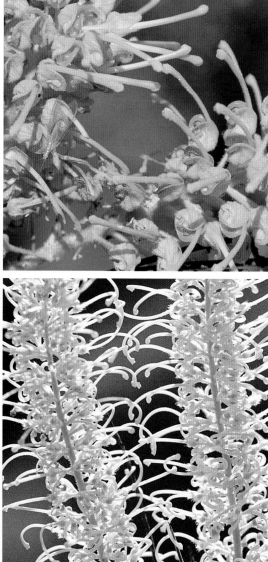

Above left: **Parrot Peas.**

Top middle: **Desert Grevillea.**

Bottom middle: **Rattlepod Grevillea.**

Top right: **Desert Fringe Myrtle.**

Bottom right: **Orange Immortelle.**

flowers and seeds. Small lizards hunt insects. Larger lizards such as the goannas hunt the smaller lizards.

Once the flowers are out, birds arrive in droves to sip the nectar, feast on seeds and catch insects and reptiles. They begin to nest immediately and raise brood after brood of chicks until the plants wither in the summer's heat.

Top left: **Mini Daisy.**

Bottom left: **Cassia.**

Top middle: **Sturt's Nightshade.**

Bottom middle: **Wallflower Poison Bush.**

Above right: **Saltspoon Daisies.**

Top: **Sand Goanna.**

Above left: **Central Netted Dragon.**

Middle right: **Thorny Devil.**

Bottom right: **One of the many species of skinks that live in these arid lands.**

Top: Katydid.

Bottom: Ants harvesting seeds.

Left: Pink Cockatoo at the entrance to its nest hollow. This bird is also known as Major Mitchell's Cockatoo.

Right: White-fronted Honeyeater gathering nectar.

Top: Male Masked Woodswallow at his nest.

Bottom: Male Crimson Chat feeds his young.

DEFENCES

The insects and reptiles are not the helpless victims of those wanting to eat them – they have many defences. Some ants have massive jaws and a painful sting. The Thorny Devil is protected by its covering of spikes. Other species rely on speed, dashing to a safe burrow at the first sign of danger.

Others again, especially among the insects, taste bad or are poisonous – something they advertise to possible attackers with their bright colours.

The best defence, however, seems to be camouflage. The colours of animals that seek protection in camouflage resemble the

Above: **A Wongai Ningaui with a grasshopper it has caught.**

rocks, sand, leaves and stems of their environment so closely that the animals are hard to see.

But every defence calls forth a predator that will penetrate it. The ningaui, for example, tracks its prey by scent, so that camouflage gives no safety at all.

Above left: **This large Bulldog Ant can give a painful sting.**

Top right: **Horned Beetle.**

Middle right: **This Earless Dragon has almost the same colour and texture as the rock of Kata Tjuta.**

Bottom right: **The Gibber Grasshopper is camouflaged among pebbles.**

EXTINCTIONS

On Uluṟu's south-east cliff is *Ikari*, a cave. One day *Tjintirtjintirpa* (Willie Wagtail) woman was in this cave. She heard songs as an *inma*, or ceremony, approached. The cave's acoustics magnified the sound and made the woman laugh – her laugh is carved in the rock in the shape of her mouth.

But *Ikari* also has a sad significance. For hundreds of years, animals' bones and teeth have accumulated. Some animals died there; others were brought by owls, dingos and other predators. Bones of about 40 species of mammals lie in the cave. Half of them are not found in central Australia any more, or have become extinct. Among those no longer found are *Ninu*, the bilby, and *Mala*, the Rufous Hare-wallaby. *Mala* is an animal of great importance in *Tjukurpa*, and its loss causes deep sadness and great concern to Aṉangu.

Left: *Ikari* Cave on the south-east of Uluṟu.

Above left: *Mala*, the Rufous Hare-wallaby.

Above right: *Ninu*, the bilby.

Shifting clouds and rain; ever-changing sunlight; towering red rocks; never-ending lines of sand dunes; changing seasons; flowers, birds and other animals; A<u>n</u>angu and *Tjukurpa* that make sense of it all – these provide the mystical moods, the impressions, the enduring images of this magical place at Australia's very heart.

Left: **A mysterious corner of Ulu<u>r</u>u during rain.**

Above: **The dead wood of a fallen tree and the flowers of the Tangled Burr Daisy are signs of death and renewal, drought and rain.**

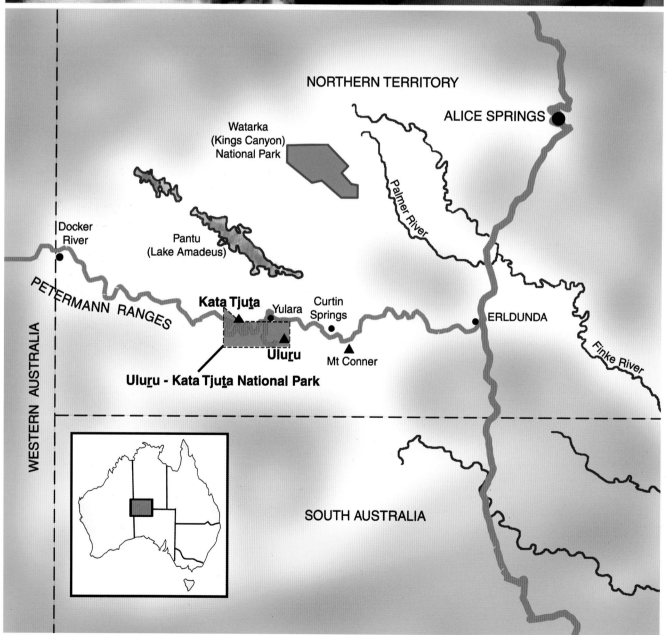

NORTHERN TERRITORY

ALICE SPRINGS

Watarka
(Kings Canyon)
National Park

Palmer River

Docker
River

Pantu
(Lake Amadeus)

PETERMANN RANGES

Kata Tjuṯa

Yulara

Curtin
Springs

ERLDUNDA

WESTERN AUSTRALIA

Uluṟu

Mt Conner

Finke River

Uluṟu - Kata Tjuṯa National Park

SOUTH AUSTRALIA

ANANGU GLOSSARY

Anangu. "The People"; the Pitjantjatjara and Yankunytjatjara peoples, who live on the plains around Uluru–Kata Tjuta. Anangu are the guardians of Uluru–Kata Tjuta.

Ili. The Rock Fig; it has edible fruit that are red when ripe.

Ilykuwara. A type of wattle; *maku* are dug from its roots.

Inma. Ceremonies; includes dances.

Kalaya. Emu.

Kali. Boomerang.

Kaliny-kaliny. Honey Grevillea bushes.

Kampurarpa. Bush Tomatoes; grow on a small bush.

Kulata. Spear.

Kuniya. Woma Python.

Liru. Any venomous snake.

Lungkata. Blue-tongued Lizard.

Maku. Witchetty grubs; caterpillars of a moth.

Mala. Rufous Hare-wallaby.

Malu. Red Kangaroo.

Mamu. A monster; invisible, but children believe *Mamus* come out at night.

Mangata. Quandong; small, tasty, bright orange-red fruit.

Milpali. Sand Goanna. (Goannas are sometimes called monitor lizards.)

Minga. General name for ants of all sorts.

Ngiyari. Thorny Devil.

Ninu. Bilby.

Panpanpalala. Crested Bellbird.

Papa. Dingo.

Piti. Wooden dishes of all shapes and sizes.

Tjala. Honey Ants.

Tjintirtjintirpa. Willie Wagtail.

Tjukurpa. The creation time of the Anangu, which gives them their Law, history and beliefs, and tells them how to live in and with the land.

Wakalpuka. A type of wattle; the seeds are ground up to make flour.

Wana. Digging stick

ENGLISH GLOSSARY

accumulate. To heap things up; to collect things.

alluvial fan. A fan-shaped mass of mud, soil, rocks and sand deposited by a river or stream when the water's flow suddenly slows down. This is usually at the bottom of a mountain or where a valley opens onto the plain.

camouflaged. Having colours or patterns that blend with rocks and plants, and so being hard to see.

circumference. The distance around the outside of something, or its outside edge.

crevice. A crack or opening.

culture. All the habits, beliefs and ways of living of a group of people; the way of life children learn.

dominate. To control or tower over something.

dormant. Still, unchanging; as if in a coma.

erode. Of the land, to wear away as a result of wind and, mainly, rain or running water.

erratic. Of rainfall, not following any pattern from one year to the next.

germinate. To sprout from seed and put out shoots.

heroic. Brave, daring and noble; like a hero.

indicator. A marker or pointer; something that shows the way, or marks a spot.

life force. Everything that gives meaning to people's lives; the power of a people's spiritual life.

magnify. To make something bigger, or to make it look bigger.

metamorphose. To change from one form into another (like a caterpillar into a moth).

monolith (*adjective* **monolithic**). A single block or piece of stone that can be natural (Uluru) or made by people (a statue).

mystical. Spiritual; strange; not part of normal, everyday life.

ningaui. A tiny marsupial that hunts insects and small lizards.

nutritious. Supplying food needed by the body; healthy.

oxidise. To change an element (metals, etc.) into its oxide. Rust is oxidised iron.

predator. An animal that hunts other animals for food.

predominant. Most common, or strongest, thing.

sedimentary rock. Rock formed when sediment is pressed together by layers of rock and dirt above it.

spawn. To lay eggs (fish or frogs, particularly).

species. A single kind of animal or plant; for example, all humans are one species.

survive. To live through some hardship.

swarm. Of insects, to fly together in large numbers.

tradition. Beliefs and customs handed down from one generation of people to the next.

INDEX

First published by Steve Parish Publishing Pty Ltd
PO Box 1058, Archerfield, Queensland 4108, Australia
www.steveparish.com.au
© copyright Stanley Breeden, 2001
Map by Kaisa Oiderman